J

D0436812

HOW TO SURVIVE A
HURRICANE

KENNY ABDO

Bolt!
An Imprint of Abdo Zoom
abdopublishing.com

abdopublishing.com

Published by Abdo Zoom, a division of ABDO, P.O. Box 398166, Minneapolis, Minnesota 55439. Copyright © 2019 by Abdo Consulting Group, Inc. International copyrights reserved in all countries. No part of this book may be reproduced in any form without written permission from the publisher. Bolt!™ is a trademark and logo of Abdo Zoom.

Printed in the United States of America, North Mankato, Minnesota.
052018
092018

THIS BOOK CONTAINS
RECYCLED MATERIALS

Photo Credits: Alamy, AP Images, iStock, Shutterstock
Production Contributors: Kenny Abdo, Jennie Forsberg, Grace Hansen
Design Contributors: Dorothy Toth, Neil Klinepier

Library of Congress Control Number: 2017960652

Publisher's Cataloging-in-Publication Data

Names: Abdo, Kenny, author.
Title: How to survive a hurricane / by Kenny Abdo.
Description: Minneapolis, Minnesota : Abdo Zoom, 2019. | Series: How to survive |
    Includes online resources and index.
Identifiers: ISBN 9781532123269 (lib.bdg.) | ISBN 9781532124242 (ebook) |
    ISBN 9781532124730 (Read-to-me ebook)
Subjects: LCSH: Survival--Juvenile literature. | Hurricanes--Juvenile literature. |
    Emergencies--Planning--Juvenile literature. | Natural disasters--
    Juvenile literature.
Classification: DDC 613.69--dc23

TABLE OF CONTENTS

HURRICANES

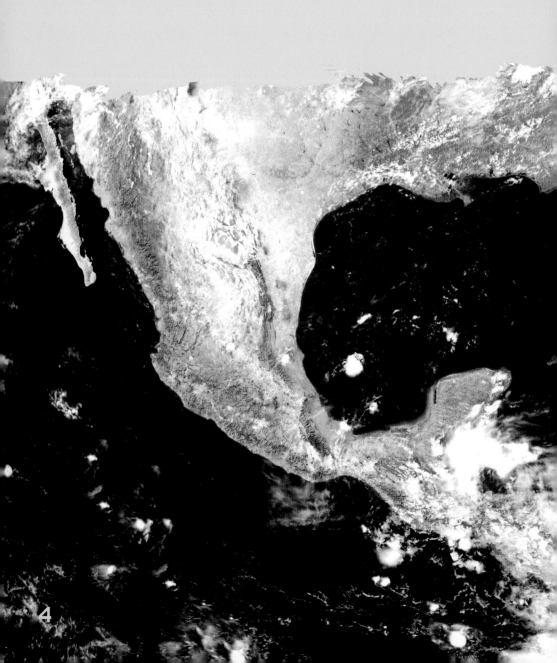

Hurricanes are giant rotating storms that can cause wind speeds of more than 160 mph (257 kph). They can release more than 2.4 trillion gallons (9 trillion liters) of rain a day.

Hurricane Irma was a very powerful hurricane that hit the **Atlantic** in 2017. It is the strongest storm on record in the open Atlantic region. It caused $64.2 billion dollars in damage.

PREPARE

Hurricane winds can cause trees and branches to fall. Before hurricane season, remove damaged trees and limbs to keep you and your home safe. Permanent storm **shutters** are the best protection for windows.

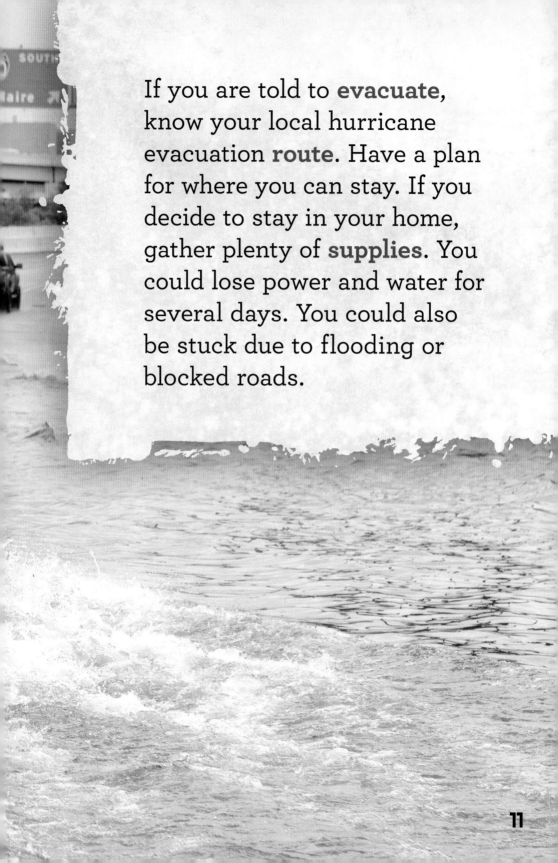

If you are told to **evacuate**, know your local hurricane evacuation **route**. Have a plan for where you can stay. If you decide to stay in your home, gather plenty of **supplies**. You could lose power and water for several days. You could also be stuck due to flooding or blocked roads.

Put together a disaster supply kit. It should include a flashlight, batteries, and first aid **supplies**. Medications, a battery-powered radio, and plenty of water will also be helpful.

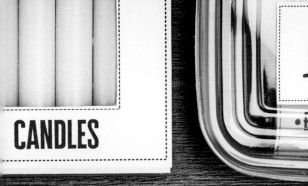

CANDLES

BATTERIES

·BATTERY·

DISASTER PREPARATION LIST

- WATER
- NON-PERISHABLE FOOD
- BATTERY RADIO
- BATTERIES
- FIRST AID KIT
- FLASHLIGHT
- BLANKET
- CANDLES
- CAN OPENER
- PRESCRIPTION MEDS
- PET FOOD
- WARM CLOTHING

- CELL PHONE
- MATCHES
- WHISTLE
- CASH & KEYS
- HAND SANITIZER
- BASIC TOOL SET
- TRASH BAGS
- BABY SUPPLIES
- EMERGENCY CONTACTS
- PERSONAL HYGIENE ITEMS
- DUST MASK
- IMPORTANT DOCS

EMERGENCY INFORMATION ....
....
....

SPARE KEYS

SURVIVE

Stay indoors during a hurricane. Close your storm **shutters**, and stay away from windows. Flying glass from broken windows can be very dangerous.

If it floods, avoid touching the floodwater. It may be filled with **sewage**. Dangerous insects or animals could also be in it.

CLUTE, TX

BREAKING NEW
EYE OF STORM HITS GALVES
110-MILE-AN-HOUR WIND
COMMUTE

Turn on your TV or battery-powered radio every 30 minutes.

ONLINE RESOURCES

Booklinks
NONFICTION NETWORK
FREE! ONLINE NONFICTION RESOURCES

To learn more about surviving a hurricane, please visit abdobooklinks.com. These links are routinely monitored and updated to provide the most current information available.

INDEX